By: Christopher Martin

Mammals of Europe, Central and North America

North America

Island Gray Fox

This is island gray fox is a small fox that is native to six of eight Channel Islands of California. There are six subspecies of this fox, each unique the island it lives on, along with its evolutionary history. Other names for this fox are coast fox, short tailed fox, channel island fox, California channel island fox and insular gray fox. The island fox shares the Urocyon genius with the mainland gray fox, the species from which it is descended from. Its small size is a result of dwarfism, because the island fox is geographically isolated, it has no immunity to parasites and diseases brought in from the mainland and is especially vulnerable to those that the domestic dog may carry. In addition, predation by the golden eagle and human activities devastated fox numbers on several of the Channel Islands in the 1990s. Four island fox subspecies were federally protected as an endangered species in 2004, and efforts to rebuild fox populations and restore the ecosystems of the Channel Islands are being undertaken. Radio collars are being attached to foxes in an effort to track

And

Locate the young foxes. To date these efforts have been largely successful.

Wolverine

The wolverine, also referred to as glutton, carcajou, skunk bear, or quick hatch, is the largest land-dwelling species. It is a stocky and muscular carnivore, more closely resembling a small bear. The wolverine, a solitary animal, has a reputation for ferocity and strength out of proportion to its size, with the documented ability to kill prey many times larger than itself .The wolverine

Can be found primarily in reaches of the Northern boreal forests, subarctic alpine. And tundra of the Northern Hemisphere, with the greatest numbers in northern Canada the U.S. state of Alaska, the Nordic countries of Europe, and throughout western Russia and Siberia. Their populations have experienced a steady decline since the 19th century in the face of trapping, range reduction and habitat fragmentation, such that they are essentially disappearing in the southern end of their European range.

Stellar Sea lion

The Stellar sea lion also known as the northern sea lion is a **near threatened** species of **sea lions** in the northern **Pacific**. It is the **sole member** of the largest of the **eared seals**. Among **pinnipeds**, it is inferior in size only to the **walrus** and the two **elephant seals**. The species is named for the naturalist **Georg Wilhelm Stellar,** who first described them in 1741. The Stellar sea lion has attracted considerable attention in recent decades due to significant, unexplained declines in their numbers over a large portion of their range in **Alaska.**

Gray wolf

The gray wolf also known as the timber wolf, or western wolf, is a candid native to the wilderness and areas of North America, Eurasia, and northern, eastern and western Africa. It is the largest extant member of its family, with males averaging 43–45 kg (95–99 lb), and females 36–38.5 kg (79–85 lb). Like the red wolf, it is distinguished from other canis species by its larger size and less pointed features, particularly on the ears and muzzle. Its winter fur is long and bushy, and predominantly a mottled gray in color, although nearly pure white, red, or brown to black also occur. As of 2005, 37 subspecies of C. lupus are recognized by MSW3. The subspecies is the Eurasian wolf, also known as the common wolf. The gray wolf is the most specialized member of the genus Canis, as demonstrated by its morphological adaptations to hunting large prey, its more gregarious nature, and it's highly advanced expressive behavior. It is nonetheless closely related enough to smaller Canis species, such as the eastern wolf, coyote and golden jackal to produce fertile hybrids. Its closest relative is the domestic dog, with which it shared a common European ancestor which likely diverged 14,900 years ago. It is the only species of Canis to have a range encompassing both the Old and New Worlds, and originated in Eurasia during the Pleistocene, colonizing North America on at least three separate occasions. It's a social animal, travelling in nuclear families consisting of a mated pair, accompanied by the pair's adult offspring. The gray wolf is typically an apex predator throughout its range, with only humans and tigers posing a serious threat to it. It feeds primarily on large hoofed animals like deer, though it also eats smaller animals, livestock, carrion, and garbage. The gray wolf is one of the world's best known and well researched animals, with probably more books written about it than any other wildlife species. It has a long history of association with humans, having been despised and hunted in most pastoral communities due to its attacks on livestock, while conversely being respected in some agrarian and hunter-gatherer societies. Although the fear of wolves is pervasive in many human societies, the majority of recorded attacks on people have been attributed to animals suffering from rabies. Non-rabid wolves have attacked and killed people, mainly children, but this is unusual, as wolves are relatively few, live away from people, and have been taught to fear humans by hunters and shepherds.

Black Footed-Ferret

The black-footed ferret, also known as the American polecat or prairie dog hunter, is a species of mustlide native to central North America. It is listed as endangered by the IUCN, because of its very small and restricted populations. First discovered by Audubon and Bachman in 1851, the species declined throughout the 20th century, primarily as a result of decreases in prairie dog populations and sylvatic plague. It was declared extinct in 1979 until Lucille Hogg's dog brought a dead black-footed ferret to her door in Meatiest, Wyoming in 1981. That remnant population of a few dozen ferrets lasted there until the animals were considered extinct in the wild in 1987. However, a captive breeding program launched by the United States Fish and Wildlife Service resulted in its reintroduction into eight western states and Mexico from 1991–2008. There are now over 1,000 mature, wild-born individuals in the wild across 18 populations, with four self-sustaining populations in South Dakota (two), Arizona and Wyoming. The black-footed ferret is roughly the size of a mink, and differs from the European polecat by the greater contrast between its dark limbs and pale body and the shorter length of its black tail-tip. In contrast, differences between the black-footed ferret and the steppe polecat of Asia are slight, to the point where the two species were once thought to be conspecific.The only noticeable differences between the black-footed ferret and the steppe polecat are the former's much shorter and coarser fur, larger ears, and longer post molar extension of the palate. It is largely nocturnal and solitary, except when breeding or raising litters. Up to 91% of its diet is composed of prairie dogs.

Europe

Stoat

The stoat, also known as the short-tailed weasel, is a species of Mustelid native to Eurasia and North America, distinguished from the least weasel by its larger size and longer tail with a prominent black tip. The name ermine is often, but not always, used for the animal in its pure white winter coat, or the fur thereof. In the late 19th century, stoats were introduced into New Zealand to control rabbits. The stoats have had a devastating effect on native bird populations. It is classed by the IUCN as Least Concern, due to its wide circumpolar distribution, and because it does not face any significant threat to its survival. It was named one of the world's top 100 "worst invasive species" by the IUCN Species Survival Commission's Invasive Species Specialist Group.

The ermine luxury fur is often used by Catholic monarchs, Pontiffs and Cardinals who sometimes use it as the mozzetta cape, and devotional images as such.

Chinese Water Deer

The water deer is a small deer superficially more similar to a musk deer than a true deer. Native to China and Korea, there are two subspecies: the Chinese water deer and the Korean water deer. Despite its lack of antlers and certain other anatomical anomalies—including a pair of prominent tusks (downward-pointing canine teeth), it is classified as a cervid. Its unique anatomical characteristics have caused it to be classified in its own genus (*Hydropotes*) as well as its own subfamily (Hydropotinae).However, a study of mitochondrial cytochrome sequences placed it near *Capreolus* within an Old World section of subfamily the Capreolinae. Its prominent tusks (elongated canines), similar to those of musk deer, have led to both being colloquially named vampire deer in English-speaking areas to which they have been imported.

Wildcat

The wildcat is a small cat found throughout most of Africa, Europe, and southwest and central Asia into India, China, and Mongolia. Because of its wide range it is classed by the IUCN Least Concern. However, crossbreeding with housecats is extensive and has occurred throughout almost the entirety of the species' range, potentially threatening the genetic diversity of the wild subspecies. The wildcat shows a high degree of geographic variation. Asiatic subspecies have spotted, isabelline coats, African subspecies have sandy-grey fur with banded legs and red-backed ears,

And European wildcats resemble heavily built striped tabbies with bushy tails, white chins and throats. All subspecies are generally larger than housecats, with longer legs and more robust bodies. The actual number of subspecies is still debated, with some organizations recognizing 22, while others recognize only four, including the Chinese mountain cat, which was previously considered a species in its own right. Genetic, morphological and archaeological evidence suggests that the house cat was domesticated from the African wildcat, probably 9,000-10,000 years ago in the Fertile Crescent region of the Near East, coincident with the rise of agriculture and the need to protect harvests stored in granaries from rodents.

Reeves's muntjac

The Reeves's muntjac is a muntjac species found widely in southeastern China and in Taiwan. They have also been introduced in Belgium, the Netherlands, the United Kingdom south England, the Midlands, and east Wales and Ireland by 2008. It feeds on herbs, blossoms, succulent shoots, grasses and nuts, and was also reported to eat trees. It takes its name from John Reeves, who was appointed Assistant Inspector of Tea for the British East India Company in 1812.

Mountain Hare

The mountain hare is a large species, though it is slightly smaller than the European hare. It grows to a length of 45–65 cm (18–26 in), with a tail of 4–8 cm (1.6–3.1 in), and a mass 2–5.3 kg (4.4–11.7 lb), females being slightly heavier than males. In summer, for all populations of mountain hares, the coat is various shades of brown. In preparation for

Winter most populations molt into a white (or largely white) pelage. The tail remains completely white all year round, distinguishing the mountain hare from the European hare, which has a black upper side to the tail. The subspecies *Lepus timidus hibernicus*, or the Irish mountain hare stays brown all year and individuals rarely develop a white coat. The Irish variety may also have a dark/grey upper surface to the tail, which in other populations always remains white. This tail color combined with its large size (in comparison to most other populations of mountain hare) and the various shades of brown that the Irish hare main display, could lead an inexperienced observer to misidentify an Irish mountain hare as a European hare.

Central America

Capybara

Capybaras are located in South America and also Panama, the most southern country of Central America. Capybaras are mostly found in dense forests near water sources such as streams, ponds, rivers, swamps and lakes. Capybaras will run to the water to escape from potential threats. Capybaras' diets consist of fruits, grasses and water plants. They will also feed on vegetables grown on farms. Capybaras are the largest rodents on earth. Adult capybaras are typically between 3 - 4 feet long and can weigh between 100 and 150 pounds. Capybaras' heads resemble those of other rodents, but are much larger. They have small ears and their legs are short compared to their round bodies. Capybaras have reddish-brown hair and two long front teeth that are typical in rodents. Capybaras are well-suited for living in and near the water. Their webbed feet make them excellent swimmers, helping to propel them through the water quickly. They also have the ability to hide under water for extended periods of time by holding their noses just above the surface. They can sit completely underwater and hold their breath for up to five minutes. Gestation or pregnancy periods of female capybaras last approximately 5 months. They will usually give birth to litters consisting of 2 - 8 offspring. Like other rodents, capybaras have two long front teeth that never stop growing. Rather, their teeth are worn down by chewing on foods or bark. Capybaras are social animals, living in groups controlled by one dominant male. They can communicate using various sounds to signal danger. Capybaras are often hunted for meat or for their hides, which make very high-quality leather. They may be killed by farmers who view them as pests for destroying crops.

Ocelots

Ocelots are one of the more beautiful feline species. Their coat is short and soft, forming two whorls on the shoulder, the hairline on the neck being directed towards the crown. Ground color varies from whitish or tawny yellow to reddish grey. Markings run into chain-like streaks and blotches, forming elongate spots bordered with black enclosing an area darker than the ground color. The head is rather large with two black cheek stripes on each side surrounding an almost white area. Irises are brown or golden. The underside is snowy white with black spots, and the tail is ringed or barred with black on the upper side, whitish on the underside, and black tipped. Relatively short, stout legs, with large padded feet, are marked with solid black spots and bars. Like most wild cats, the backs of the rounded ears are black with a white central spot.

Orca

The orca, or killer whale, with its striking black and white coloring, is one of the best known of all the cetaceans. It has been extensively studied in the wild and is often the main attraction at many sea parks and aquaria. A toothed whale, the orca is known for being a carnivorous, fast and skillful hunter, with a complex social structure and a cosmopolitan distribution (orcas are found in all the oceans of the world). Sometimes called "the wolf of the sea", the orca can be a fierce hunter with well-organized hunting techniques, although there are no documented cases of killer whales attacking a human in the wild. Males can grow as large as 32 feet (9.6 m) long and weigh 8 to 9 tons. Females can reach 23 feet (8.2 m) in length and weigh up to 4 tons. The orca is found in all the oceans of the world, though they are more abundant in cooler waters. Unlike some other species of whales, which follow a regular migration route each year, the orca seems to travel according to the availability of food. They are one of the few species of whales that move freely from hemisphere to hemisphere.

Giant Ant Eater

Anteaters are edentate animal, they have no teeth. Their long tongues are more than sufficient to lap up the 35,000 ants and termites they swallow whole each day. The anteater uses its sharp claws to tear an opening into an anthill and put its long snout and efficient tongue to work. But it has to eat quickly, flicking its tongue up to 160 times per minute. Ants fight back with painful stings, so an anteater may spend only a minute feasting on each mound. Anteaters never destroy a nest, preferring to return and feed again in the future. These animals find their quarry not by sight theirs is poor but by smell. Anteaters are found in Central and South America, where they prefer tropical forests and grasslands. There are four different species which vary greatly in size. The silky anteater is the size of a squirrel, while the giant anteater can reach 7 feet long from the tip of its snout to the end of its tail. Some anteaters, the silky anteater, ply their trade in the trees. They travel from branch to branch in search of tasty insects. Anteaters are generally solitary animals. Females have a single offspring once a year, which can sometimes be seen riding on its mother's back. Anteaters are not aggressive but they can be fierce. A cornered anteater will get up on its hind legs, using its tail for balance, and lash out with dangerous claws. The giant anteater's claws are some four inches long, and the animal can fight off even a puma or jaguar.

Humpback Whale

The humpback whale is a species of baleen whale. Adults range in length from 12–16 meters and weigh approximately 36,000 kilograms or 79,000 lbs. The humpback has a distinctive body shape, with unusually long pectoral fins and a knobby head. An acrobatic animal known for breaching and slapping the water with its tail and fins, it is popular with whale watchers off the coasts of Australasia and the Americas. Males produce a complex song lasting 10 to 20 minutes, which they repeat for hours at a time. Its purpose is not clear, though it may have a role in mating. Found in oceans and seas around the world, humpback whales typically migrate up to 25,000 kilometers or 16,000 mi each year. Humpbacks feed only in summer, in polar waters, and migrate to tropical or subtropical waters to breed and give birth in the winter. During the winter, humpbacks fast and live off their fat reserves. Their diet consists mostly of krill and small fish. Humpbacks have a diverse repertoire of feeding methods, including the bubble net feeding technique. Like other large whales, the humpback was and is a target for the whaling industry. Once hunted to the brink of extinction, its population fell by an estimated 90% before a moratorium was introduced in 1966. While stocks have since partially recovered, entanglement in fishing gear, collisions with ships, and noise pollution continue to impact the 80,000 humpbacks worldwide.

Snow Leopard

Snow leopard is a relative species to more widely seen Leopard. It is in the same size range as leopard. Snow leopards are highly adapted to their natural habitat of cold high mountains. With their whitish-, yellowish or smoky grey fur, patterned with dark grey rosettes and spots, they can perfectly camouflage against the mountainous rocky terrain.
The fur has long hair with dense, woolly under fur to protect them against the cold environment. Snow leopards molt twice a year, but the summer coat differs little from the

winter in density and length. Snow leopards have long tails, up to 1 m in length that helps in keeping balance and as an additional protection against the cold to wrap around the body when the snow leopard is resting. Snow leopards are sparsely distributed across 12 countries in Central Asia: China, Bhutan, Nepal, India, Pakistan, Afghanistan, Tajikistan, Uzbekistan, Kyrgyzstan, Kazakhstan, Russia, and Mongolia. China contains as much as 60% of the snow leopard's habitat. The snow leopard is endangered throughout its 12 range states in Asia and is listed as 'endangered' in IUCN's Red List of Threatened Species. Human conflict is a key factor affecting the survival of the snow leopard. Snow leopards are often killed by local farmers because they prey on livestock such as sheep, goats, horses, and yak calves. In some areas domestic animals can make up to 58% of the snow leopard's diet. The reason for the snow leopard's increased reliance on domestic animals for meat is due to the decline in their natural prey base. The animals they would typically hunt such as the Argali sheep are also hunted by local communities. Much of the population decline is also attributed to hunting for the much coveted fur and for bones which are used in Chinese medicines. The habitat of the snow leopard continues to decline as increased grazing and human settlements fragment the historic range of the species.

Nine banded armadillo

Dressed in a suit of armor, the head, body, legs and tail of the nine-banded armadillo are protected by a large number of bony plates. Armadillos spend most of their time in burrows under the ground. Accordingly, their sense of smell far out-powers their vision and hearing. About the size of a domestic cat, these creatures have elongated, pointed noses and long, sticky tongues used for catching insects. Their short, strong legs have sharp claws that come in handy when digging burrows. Found from South and Central America to Oklahoma, the armadillo tends to live in forests near swampy areas. These adaptive creatures can live anywhere that is warm and has plenty of food. They prefer rainforests, temperate forests, savannas and grasslands where the soil is good for digging burrows. Armadillos can hold their breath for six minutes. When crossing a body of water armadillos can either inflate their stomachs and intestines with air and float across, or sink down to the bottom and use their claws to walk across. Armadillos' favorite foods are insects. Their special tongue allows them to consume up to 40,000 ants in one meal! They also enjoy feeding on small animals, bird eggs, roots, fruits and even rotting animal flesh (called "carrion").When startled, armadillos can jump three to four feet in the air. Even with their suit of armor, bears, coyotes, wild cats, foxes and dogs feed on armadillos. But cars continue to pose the biggest threat, and many are killed crossing the road each year. Loss of habitat is forcing increasing interactions between people and armadillos, further threatening the survival of these curious-looking creatures.